WORLD WAR I
HISTORY ILLUSTRATED IN
300 PHOTOS

Claudio Blanc

Camelot
EDITORA

President: Paulo Roberto Houch
MTB 0083982/SP

Editorial Coordination: Priscilla Sipans and Paola Houch
Art Coordination: Rubens Martim
Graphic Design: Renato Darim Parisotto
Image Selection: Claudio Blanc
Translation: Suellen Durães
English text review: Francine Oliveira
Images: Wikicommons
Sales: Phone: +55 (11) 3393-7723 (vendas@editoraonline.com.br)

Legal deposit has been made.

International Data of Cataloging in Publication (CIP) according to ISBD	
C181w	Camelot Editora World War I: History illustrated in 300 photos/ Camelot Editora.– Barueri : Camelot Editora, 2024. 160 p. ; 15.1 x 23 in. ISBN: 978-65-6095-130-3 1. Photography. I. Title.
2023-2187	CDD 770 CDU 77
Elaborated by Odilio Hilario Moreira Junior - CRB-8/9949	

Rights reserved to
IBC – Instituto Brasileiro de Cultura LTDA
CNPJ 04.207.648/0001-94
Avenida Juruá, 762 — Alphaville Industrial
Zip Code: 06455-010 – Barueri/SP
www.editoraonline.com.br

PRELUDE
TO WAR

The First World War, the largest and bloodiest conflict to date, has its origins well before 1914 and involves the intricate relationships between European powers. The role of the Austro-Hungarian Empire as a catalyst for the war was fundamental. However, the attack that assassinated Archduke Ferdinand of Austria was just the trigger that ignited the tremendously volatile atmosphere in Europe at the end of the 19th century and the beginning of the 20th.

French Emperor Napoleon III (left) as a prisoner of Bismarck (right) in the Franco-Prussian War of the 1870s: the rivalry between the two countries prepared the mood for a new confrontation.

Wikicommons/ Xiaphias

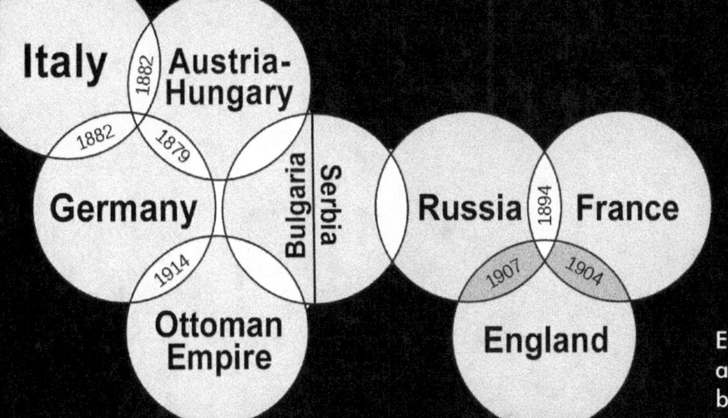

European diplomatic alignments shortly before the war.

A 1909 cartoon from Punck magazine shows the United States, Germany, Great Britain, France, and Japan involved in a naval race represented as "unlimited" gambling: the arms race was another factor that led to the conflict.

The competition resulting from the new imperialism, the period between the end of the 19th century and the beginning of the 20th century in which the European powers, the USA, and Japan sought colonial expansion, is among the causes of the First War, in the mid-1910s (a caricature from Punch magazine showing Cecil Rhodes as the colossus of Rhodes over Africa, December 1892).

Royal Navy HMS Dreadnought, the world's first dreadnought (1906). This type of vessel launched a new concept of naval warfare and had its design copied by navies around the world.

King George V (left) inspects HMS Neptune, a ship that became part of the Grand Fleet after the beginning of the First World War.

"Are we afraid? NO!" Canadian cartoon (c. 1914).

This Austrian caricature from 1914 shows the Empire as the "threshing floor of Europe."

Citizens of Sarajevo read the proclamation of the country's annexation to the Austro-Hungarian Empire in 1908 – an action that heightened political tensions in central Europe and ended up, among other factors, leading to war.

This John Bernard Partridge's cartoon published in *Punch* magazine (c. 1904) shows the German point of view of the Entente Cordiale of 1904: John Bull, the British personification, walks arm in arm with a Marianne, the symbol of the French Republic, dressed in a scandalously short skirt for the time, while the German pretends not to care.

The tendencies of this intricate network of alliances were well illustrated in a caricature published in an American magazine in 1914. The caption of the "Friendship Network" reads: "if Austria attacks Serbia, Russia makes a move on Austria, Germany on Russia, and England and France on Germany."

Kaiser Wilhelm II, in 1902: Germany promised to support Austria if it was attacked by Russia because of its policy in the Balkans.

In this caricature, the rulers of Germany, France, Russia, Austria-Hungary, and the United Kingdom try to keep the lid on the boiling cauldron of tensions to avoid a general European war.

CAUSES

The reasons that motivated the First World War go far beyond the assassination of Francisco Ferdinand and comprise national and economic policies, as well as territorial, ethnic, and cultural conflicts, in addition to a web of alliances that had been taking shape between the powers of Europe since 1870. These were some of the most important causes:

✔ The rise of nationalism throughout Europe.
✔ Territorial issues.
✔ An intricate alliance system.
✔ The shift in the balance of power between the European dominances.
✔ Fragmented governments.
✔ Delays and errors in diplomatic communication.
✔ The arms race that began in previous decades.
✔ The competition for colonies rich in raw materials.
✔ Military, economic, industrial, and commercial competition.
✔ The need, especially for France, Germany, and Austria, to overcome internal stagnation through external achievements.

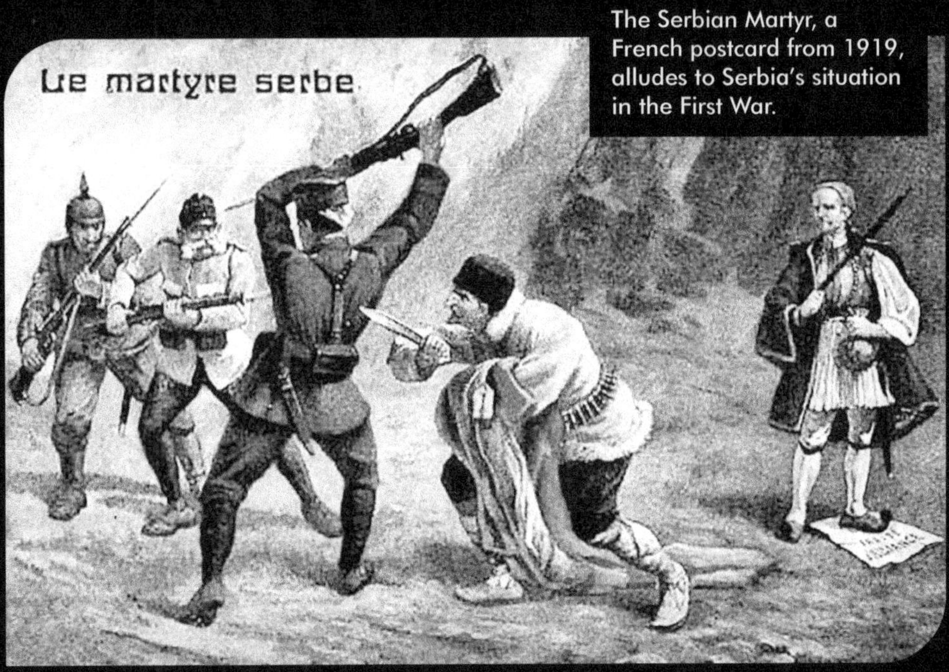

The Serbian Martyr, a French postcard from 1919, alludes to Serbia's situation in the First War.

The Archduke Franz Ferdinand in 1914. His assassination by Serbian radical Gavrilo Princip triggered the war.

Sophie, the Duchess of Hohenberg, wife of Franz Ferdinand.

The Archduke Franz Ferdinand with his wife Sophie, Duchess of Hohenberg, and their three children. Sophie was also murdered in the attack promoted by the Black Hand organization.

The ceremonial cross of the Serbian terrorist organization Black Hand.

The conspirators Trifko Grabež, Nedeljko Čabrinović, and Gavrilo Princip in Kalemegdan, Belgrade, May 1914.

The arrest of Gavrilo Princip.

Gavrilo Princip in his cell, in the Fortress of Terezín.

Gavrilo Princip, seated in the center, front row, during the trial in Sarajevo, December 1914.

1914
THE FIRST BATTLES

A studio shot of an Austrian soldier in field uniform (c. 1914).

A French attack using bayonet (c. 1914).

BATTLE OF LIÈGE |AUGUST 4-16|

The battle that opened the First World War also marked the opening of the German offensive – the invasion of Belgium. The attacks began on August 5, 1914, and ended on August 16, with the surrender of the last Belgian fort.

Belgian troops defend the suburb of Herstal, near Liège.

The Fort de Loncin shortly after the battle.

German troops at the Prince-Bishops' Palace of Liège.

BATTLE OF THE FRONTIERS | AUGUST 14–24 |

Fought along the eastern border of France and southern Belgium, the victor was Germany, whose soldiers invaded northern France through Belgium.

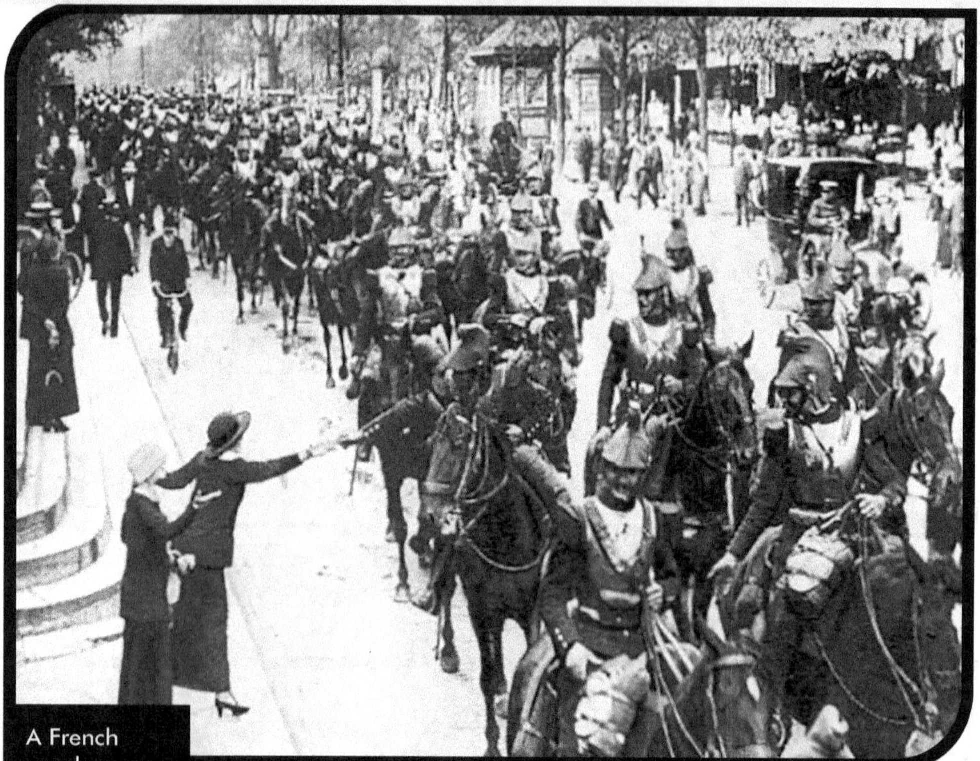

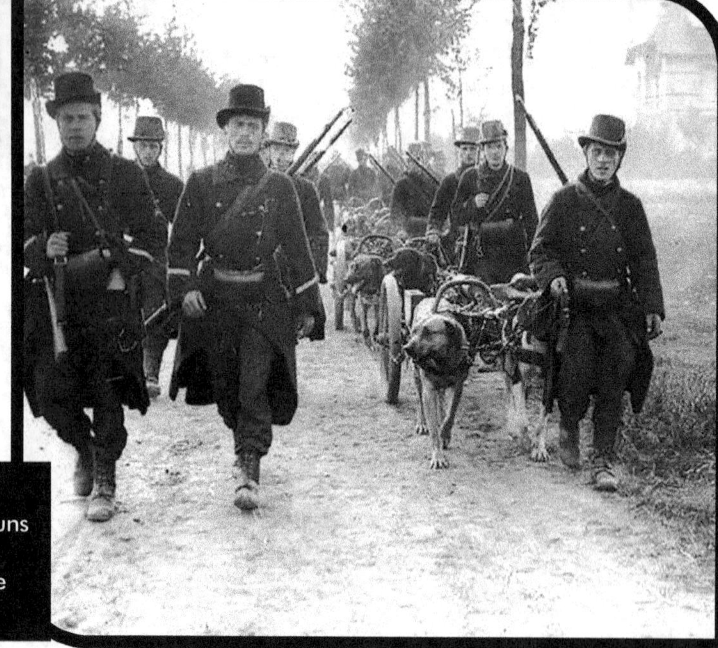

A French cavalry parade on their way to the Battle of the Frontiers, in Paris, August 1914.

Belgian troops with machine guns carried by dogs, during the Battle of the Frontiers.

The Battle of Morhange, part of the Battle of the Frontiers, as seen by French propaganda in 1915.

French equipment abandoned near Vergaville.

"Bravo, Belgium!" This political cartoon in Punch magazine, in the December 1914 issue, shows a Belgian farmer facing the German aggressor. In fact, Belgium and its population suffered heavy war crimes perpetrated by the Germans.

French prisoners in August 1914, in Sarrebourg.

BATTLE OF STALLUPÖNEN

Considered the first battle on the Eastern Front of the First World War, it was fought on August 17 between the Russian and German armies. The German victory resulted in a delay in the Russian planning schedule.

The marks of battles in Stallupönen.

BATTLE OF THE ARDENNES

This combat was among the first ones in the First World War and it was considered part of the Battle of the Frontiers.

Joseph Joffre, commander of the French army, who oversaw operations during the Battle of the Ardennes

Prince Wilhelm,
leader of the
German 5th Army.

A highlight of the location
of the Ardennes mountains,
between Belgium, France,
and Luxembourg.

Also considered part of the Battle of the Frontiers, it was the first engagement of the British Expeditionary Force (BEF).

The "A" Company of the 4th Battalion, Royal Fusiliers (City of London Regiment), part of the 9th Brigade of the 3rd Division, resting in the city square of Mons before entering the line of the Battle of Mons. The Royal Fusiliers faced some of the heaviest fighting of the battle.

Alexander von Kluck, commander of the German First Army in Mons.

British troops retreating after the battle of Mons.

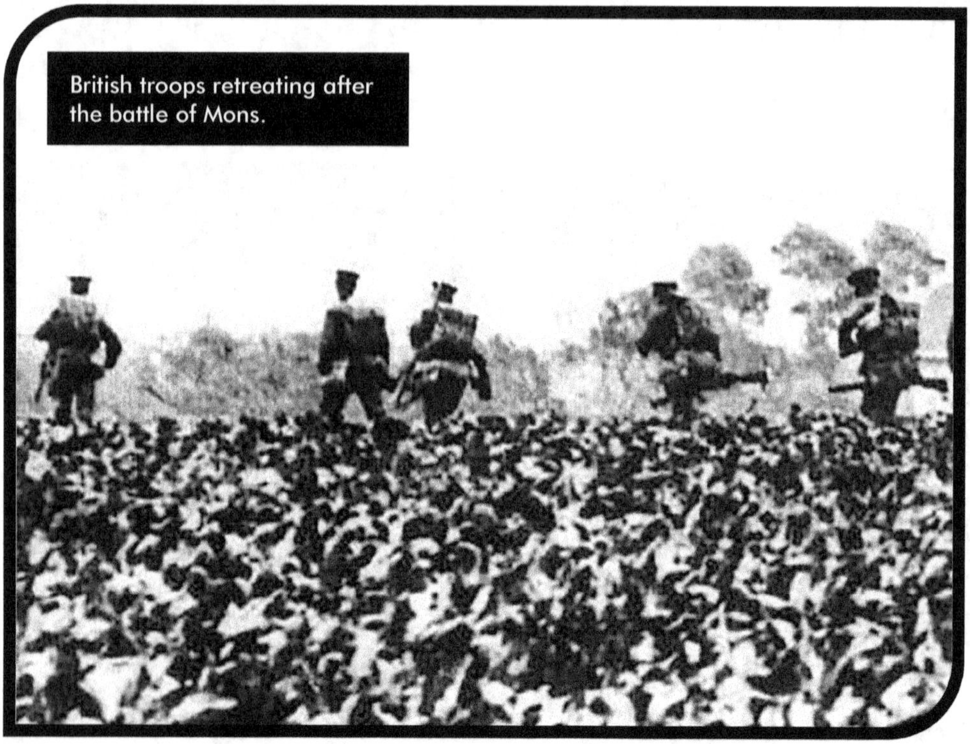

BATTLE OF TANNENBERG

AUGUST 26–30

Taking place in East Prussia between the German and Russian armies, this battle saw Germany victorious as the Germans surrounded and destroyed the Tsar's forces that had invaded East Prussia.

Russian prisoners after the Battle of Tannenberg.

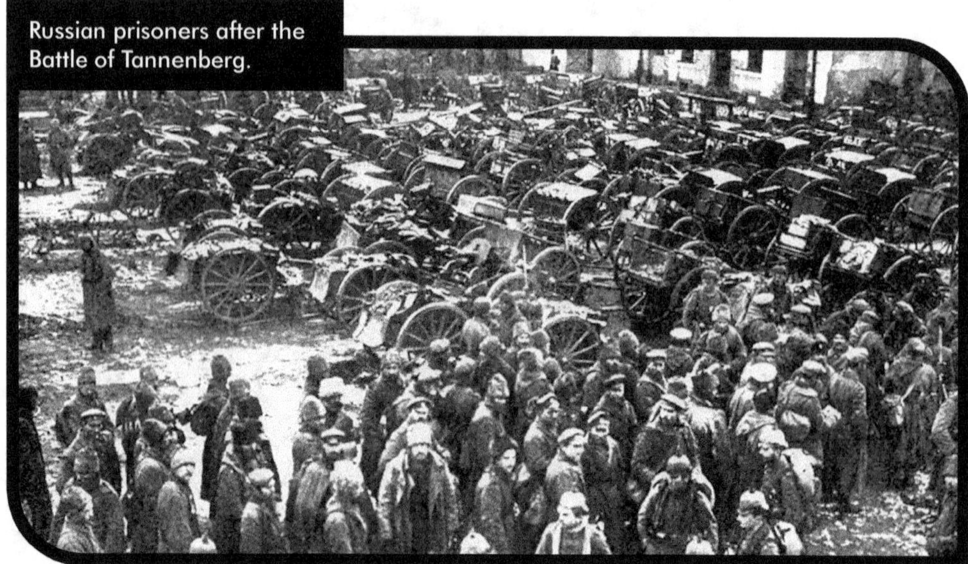

Hermann von François (with his back to the camera) imprisons Russian General Kluyev, head of the XIII Corps of the Russian Army, on August 31, 1914.

Conception of German propaganda by the duo of leaders Hindenburg and Ludendorff, by Hugo Vogel (c. 1914).

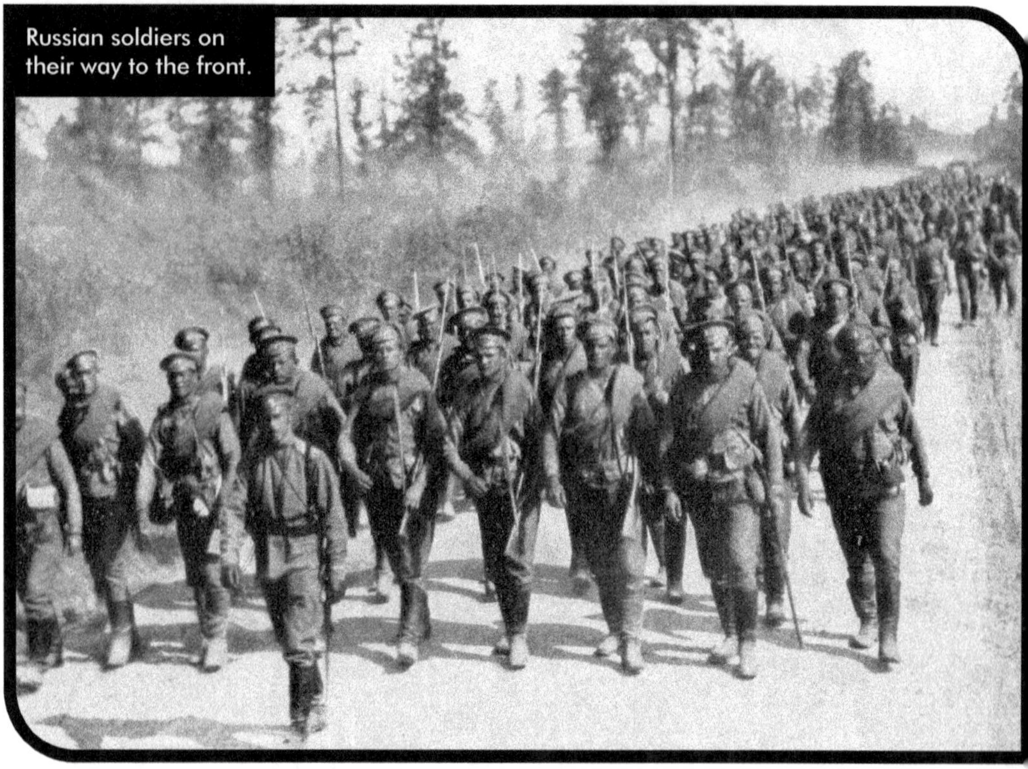

Russian soldiers on their way to the front.

BATTLE OF KRAŚNIK

AUGUST 23–25

The Austria-Hungary's first victory in World War I happened with the Austro-Hungarian 1st Army facing and defeating the Russian 4th Army.

Austro-Hungarian troops rest during the advance.

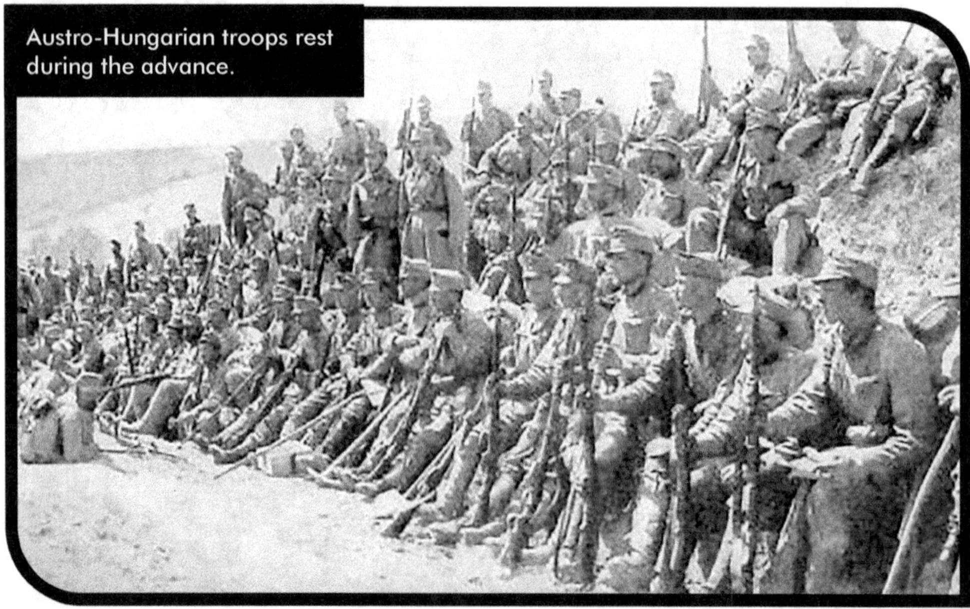

A drawing of the Austrian Dragoons at Kraśnik.

SIEGE OF MAUBEUGE | AUGUST 24 – SEPTEMBER 7 |

This clash resulted in the surrender of the French garrisons to German troops.

A French fortress ruined after German capture.

German soldiers at the
entrance to Maubeuge,
September 1914.

The remains of a tower of the
Maubeuge fortress after more
than eight days of German
bombardment with 210, 305,
and 420mm cannon.

The Maubeuge lock in 1915.

BATTLE OF LE CATEAU | AUGUST 26 |

Fought shortly after the withdrawal of British, French, and Belgian troops from the Battle of Mons, who sought to establish defensive positions in northern France.

British killed at the Battle of Le Cateau.

General Horace Smith-Dorrien commanded the British forces at Le Cateau.

BATTLE OF SAINT-QUENTIN | AUGUST 29–30 |

A confrontation involving German and French troops during the retreat of the allies from Le Cateau.

Soldiers of the French 48th Infantry Regiment in battle.

A monument erected in honor of the French 5th Army in the city of Guise.

Karl von Bülow, commander of the German 2nd Army that fought at Saint-Quentin.

FIRST BATTLE OF THE MARNE | SEPTEMBER 5–12 |

The Franco-British victory over Germany in this battle was one of the decisive moments of the First World War.

French combatants awaiting enemy assault in a trench (c. 1914).

The bayonet charge of the French infantry.

Léon Broquet painting: the Petit Morin, in the region of the battle, full of corpses on September 10, 1914.

Bodies of German soldiers killed on the battlefield, in Fère Champenoise, Marne department, France, 1914.

The transmissions between command and troops were difficult: advances were too fast for cable transmission, while radio stations had short ranges.

Lombard Street, in Sermaize-les-Bains, after the Battle of the Marne.

Special edition of *J'ai vui* magazine celebrating the victory in Marne.

French cavalry leading German prisoners.

THE RACE TO THE SEA

After Germany failed in the First Battle of the Marne, the opposing armies tried, on several occasions, to outflank each other. This phase of the war became known as "The Race to the Sea," which led to the formation of an extensive continuous line of trenches on the western front.

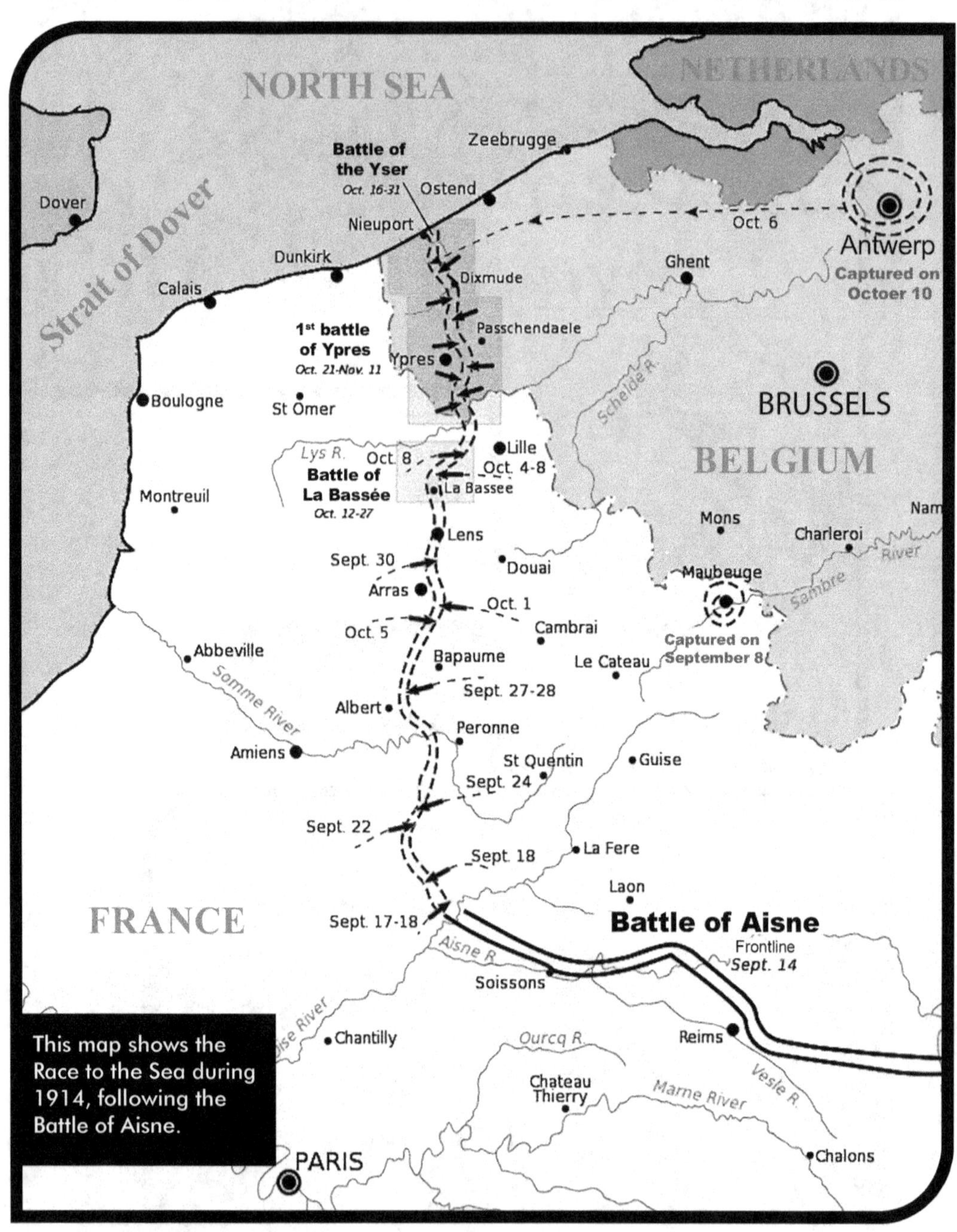

This map shows the Race to the Sea during 1914, following the Battle of Aisne.

BATTLE OF CER

It was one of the unsuccessful attempts by the Austro-Hungarian Empire to invade Serbia in the first year of the First World War, in addition to being known as the first defeat of the Central Powers.

Austro-Hungarian troops deployed to Serbia via Sarajevo.

BATTLE OF THE DRINA RIVER

The Battle of the Drina River ended in an Austro-Hungarian victory over Serbia.

Serbian cavalry in the battle of the Drina River in the village of Yagar, in early September 1914.

Serbian troops on their way to the battle of the Drina River.

FIRST BATTLE OF THE MASURIAN LAKE | SEPTEMBER 9 – 14 |

Occurring a week after the Battle of Tannenberg, this confrontation disrupted Russia's plans for the spring of 1915. It was fought on the eastern front and ended with the expulsion of the Russian First Army from East Prussia.

Members of the German 8th Army during the battle.

Generals Hindenburg and Ludendorff, commanders of the German 8th Army.

Russian prisoners at the Tilsit station (Berliner Illustrierte Zeitung: September 27, 1914).

SIEGE OF ANTWERP | SEPTEMBER 28 – OCTOBER 10 |

This battle took place between German forces and Belgian, British, and French troops. German soldiers surrounded a garrison of Belgian troops, the Belgian land army, and the British Naval Division in Antwerp following the Belgian invasion in August 1914. However, Belgian fighters disrupted Germany's plans to send soldiers to France.

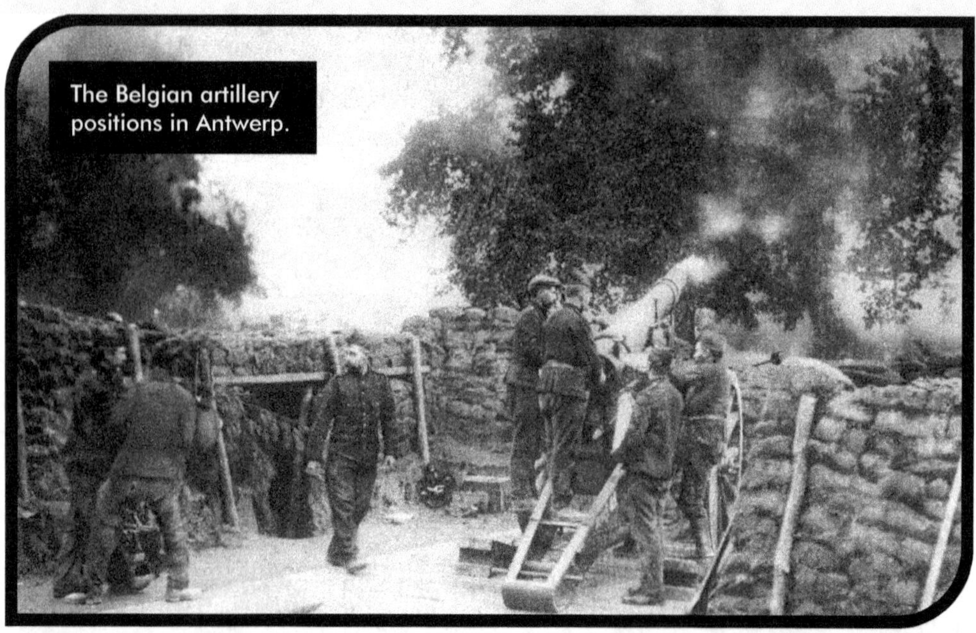

The Belgian artillery positions in Antwerp.

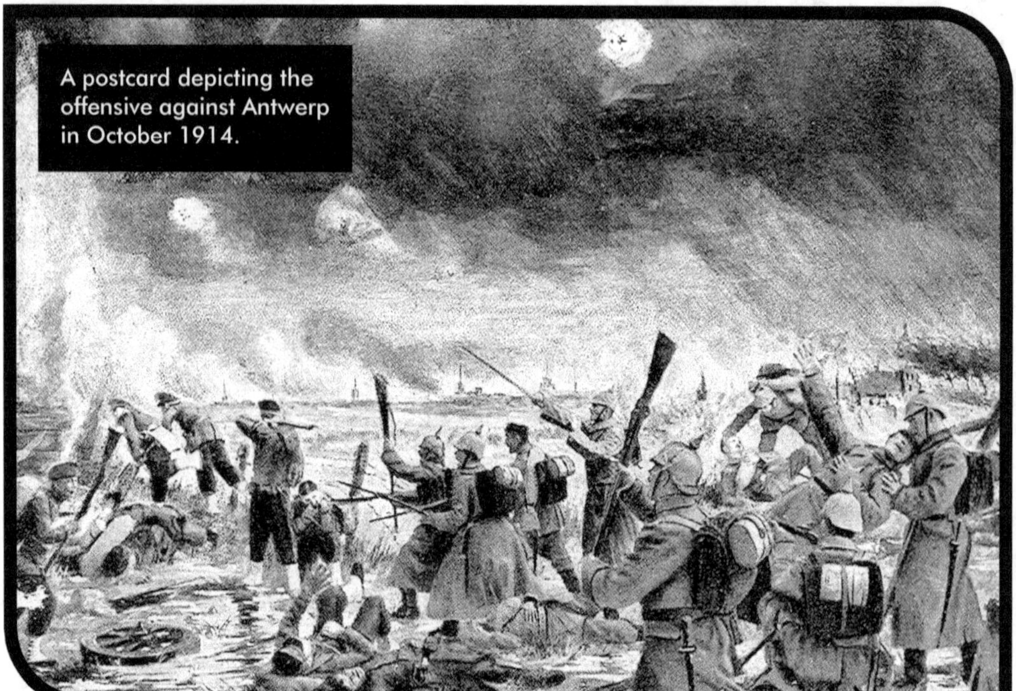

A postcard depicting the offensive against Antwerp in October 1914.

Postal propaganda for the conquest of Antwerp, October 1914.

Death workers: a 7.7cm Feldkanone 96 and its operating team.

Belgian soldiers in Antwerp in 1914.

The Big Bertha cannon, used to bombard the Antwerp forts in 1914.

A German Zeppelin during the bombing of Antwerp, on the night of August 25th and early morning of August 26th, 1914.

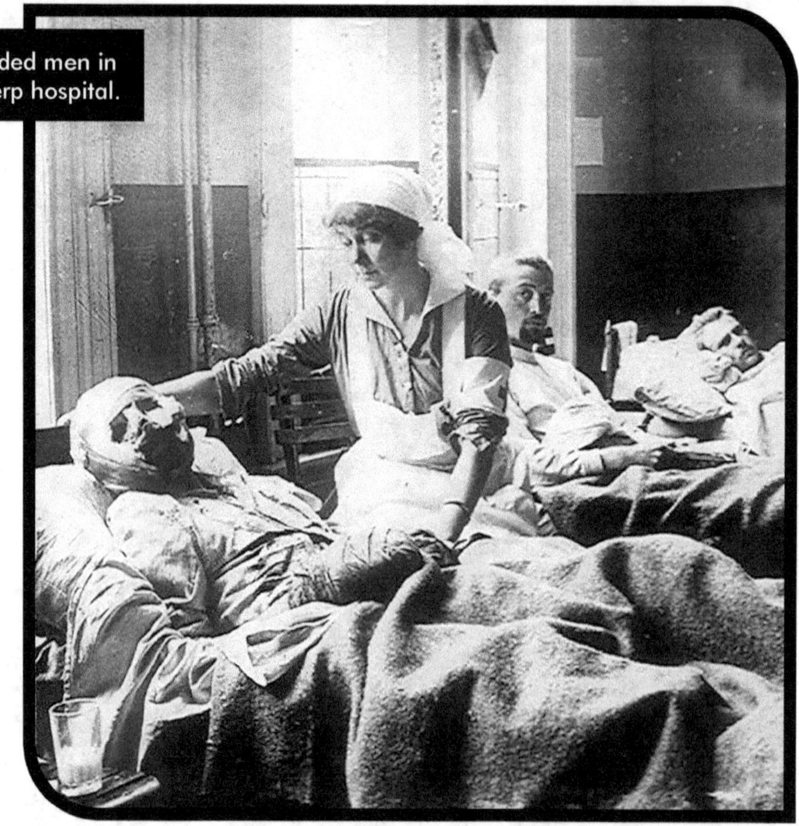

Belgian and British soldiers attempt to reach Antwerp by boat, oil painting by Willy Stöwer.

Wounded men in Antwerp hospital.

BATTLE OF THE VISTULA RIVER OR BATTLE OF WARSAW
| SEPTEMBER 29 – OCTOBER 31 |

This confrontation ended with a victory for Russia over the German Empire on the Eastern Front.

Russian soldiers cross the Vistula River in 1914.

Russian soldiers who fought on the Vistula.

THE FIRST BATTLE OF ARRAS | OCTOBER 1 – 4 |

It was an attempt by the French army to outflank the German army to prevent it from advancing to the English Channel during the Race to the Sea. However, the French failed and, on October 4, they ended up losing Lens, which allowed German soldiers to advance further north, towards Flanders.

German soldiers guarding the entrance to a frontline trench.

BATTLE OF THE YSER | OCTOBER 16 – 31 |

The line of this battle, which extended 22 miles from the Yser River to the Yperlee Canal in Belgium, was strongly defended by the Belgian army contingent, which, despite heavy casualties, halted the German advance. The victory allowed the Belgians to take control of a small part of the territory.

The "End of the Line:" the Western Front reaches the sea near Nieuwpoort, Belgium.

A depiction by A. Tolmer of German soldiers fleeing Belgian forces in the Battle of the Yser.

French marines at Yser.

FIRST BATTLE OF YPRES |OCTOBER 19 – NOVEMBER 24|

It was the last major battle at the beginning of the First War. Due to the stagnation of trench warfare, the German high command thought of breaking the enemy's device and guaranteeing victory over the Allies. To this end, he bet on an offensive in the autumn of 1914; however, the attack resulted in the deaths of more than one hundred thousand German men, many of whom were his commanders. The front was stable at the cut of the River Yser and its southern channel.

A representation of the 2nd Nonne Bosschen Company defeating the Prussian Guard in 1914 (by W. B. Wollen).

BATTLE OF ŁÓDŹ

Fought near the city of Łódź, in Poland, the combat took place between the German Ninth Army and the Russian First, Second, and Fifth Armies in terrible winter conditions, ending in an advantage for the Germans.

German soldiers in Łódź, December 1914.

German troops taking the city of Łódź.

BATTLE OF CORONEL

This naval battle took place near the city of Coronel, on the Chilean coast. Under the command of Vice Admiral Maximilian von Spee, the Imperial German Navy defeated a British Royal Navy squadron led by Rear Admiral Christopher Cradock. The shock caused by the British defeat led the United Kingdom to send more ships to the Pacific Ocean.

German squadron leaving Valparaíso on November 3, 1914, after the battle. SMS Scharnhorst and SMS Gneisenau lead the group, followed by SMS Nürnberg. In the background are the Chilean cruisers Esmeralda, O'Higgins, Blanco Encalada, and the heavy cruiser Capitán Prat.

The Battle of Coronel in a painting by Hans Bohrdt.

BATTLE OF KOLUBARA

In the Battle of Kolubara, fought between the armies of Serbia and Austria-Hungary, the Serbs emerged victorious, repelling the Austro-Hungarian army beyond their borders.

The Royal Albrecht von Württemberg 73rd Infantry Regiment at the Battle of Kolubara in December 1914.

Serbian soldiers crossing the Kolubara River.

Serbian troops on the march, c. 1914.

Austro-Hungarian soldiers next to captured pieces of Serbian artillery.

Serbian fighters on the island of Ada Ciganlija, in Belgrade.

BATTLE OF THE FALKLANDS | DECEMBER 8 |

After the defeat at the Battle of Coronel by the Germans on November 1, the British threw a large force after the German squadron. The confrontation was called "the Battle of the Falklands" and resulted in the victory of the British Royal Navy.

The cruiser SMS Gneisenau sunk in the Battle of the Falkland Islands.

A naval clash during the Battle of the Falklands in 1914. Work by William Lionel Wyllie.

The Inflexible in the rescue of survivors from Gneisenau, shortly after 6 p.m.

BATTLE OF GIVENCHY

Part of the First Battle of Champagne, the fighting around the village of Givenchy had the support of Indian troops.

Indian reinforcements who fought at Givenchy, December 1914.

FIRST BATTLE OF CHAMPAGNE

| DECEMBER 20, 1914 – MARCH 17, 1915 |

It was the first significant attack by Allied troops against the Germans since the beginning of Trench Warfare, established after the Race to the Sea.

Waiting for the attack in the trenches.

BATTLE OF SARIKAMISH

Taking place on the eastern front, it involved the armies of the Russian and Ottoman empires, resulting in Russian victory. The Ottoman forces suffered heavy casualties as they could not withstand the winter conditions of the mountains.

Russian troops in the forest in Sarikamish.

Turkish machine gun positions on the Eastern Front in early 1915.

The Armenian battalion in Sarikamish.

Members of the Ottoman 3rd Army.

A Russian propaganda
poster celebrating the battle.

Nushan Sahagian, a
13-year-old Armenian
volunteer who won a
medal for his bravery
in Sarikamish.

1915

THE BATTLE OF DOGGER BANK | JANUARY 24 |

Fought between British and German squadrons on Dogger's Bank in the North Sea, this naval battle resulted in a significant British victory. After suffering several attacks from British warships, the Germans lost the cruiser Blücher and most of its crew.

German cruisers (L-R) Derfflinger, Moltke, and Seydlitz en route to Dogger Bank.

The SMS Blücher rolls onto its side in its sinking state as the crew tries to hold on to the cruiser's hull.

BATTLE OF NEUVE CHAPELLE | MARCH 10 – 13 |

The Battle of Neuve Chapelle was a British offensive in the Artois region that broke through the German defenses at Neuve-Chapelle, but the British were unable to exploit the advantage they gained.

Battlefield sacrifice: a German soldier killed at Neuve Chapelle.

SECOND BATTLE OF YPRES | APRIL 22 – MAY 25 |

The various battles the troops of France, the United Kingdom, Australia, and Canada fought against the German Empire featured, for the first time, the use of hydrochloric gas as a weapon of war, launched by German forces. It was also the first time a colonial force (Canadians and Australians) faced a European power on European soil.

A night photo of a German barrage to the Allied trenches at Ypres (probably taken during the 2nd Battle of Ypres).

Ruins of the Ypres market square, after the second battle.

Part of a set of photographs taken by Frank Hurley showing the Australian battery in action with a 9.2-inch Howitzer gun (Western Front, Ypres area, Belgium).

Royal Marine Artillery machine gun crew discharging a 15-inch Howitzer gun in the Ypres Sector. These warheads weigh around 1,400 lb, and their explosion opens an average crater more than sixteen feet deep and forty-nine feet in diameter, throwing shrapnel and fragments across a radius of more than 2,620 feet. The dog sitting on one of the warheads was adopted by the gunners and used to sleep under the cannon at night.

GALLIPOLI CAMPAIGN
| FEBRUARY 17, 1915 – JANUARY 9, 1916 |

Also called the Battle or Campaign of the Dardanelles, it took place on the Gallipoli peninsula (Turkey) and is considered one of the bloodiest campaigns of the Great War. British, French, Australian, and New Zealand forces landed in Gallipoli, in an attempt to invade Turkey and capture the Dardanelles, but the attempt failed, with many deaths on both sides. The Allies retreated between December 1915 and January 1916. The ANZAC (Australian and New Zealand Army Corps) divisions were especially harmed and accused British officers of arrogance, cruelty, and ineptitude.

Mustafa Kemal (Atatürk) in the trenches of Gallipoli during the First World War. After the war, Kemal was the founder of the Republic of Turkey.

A British soldier at a colleague's grave near Cape Helles, Gallipoli (11/1/1915).

ANZAC divisions land at Gallipoli, 1915.

The Allied troops disembark.

Wounded ANZAC soldiers being rescued.

British riflemen leave the trenches for a bayonet charge against the Turks at Gallipoli.

Field Marshal Kitchener and General Birdwood inspect the front on November 15, 1915, during the Gallipoli Campaign.

The Dardanelles fleet.

Minesweeping in the Dardanelles in 1915 by British and French troops.

The sinking of the ship Bouvet in the Dardanelles, as conceived by Diyarbakir Tahsin Bey.

French troops arriving on the Greek island Lemnos in 1915 during the Gallipoli Campaign.

German heavy artillery
in Gallipoli (1915).

Turkish machine gun position
with German officers assisting in
fighting in the Dardanelles, Turkey.

Turkish heavy artillery shells the British Mavro observation post on Rabbit Island at the entrance to the Dardanelles Strait (1915).

A British 127mm ("60 pounder") cannon firing at Ottoman positions at Cape Helles, June 1915.

A British machine gun equipped with a periscope.

A French soldier leaving the trench during an attack on the Dardanelles.

Photograph taken at Anzac during the 24 May 1915 truce arranged to recover and bury fallen bodies in "no man's land," as the unoccupied space between enemy trenches was called.

The Ottoman commander of the Dardanelles Campaign, Esat Pasha, gives orders to the artillery batteries at Anzac Cove.

Australian Lieutenant General Sir Leslie James Morshead, whose military career spanned both world wars, in a trench after the battle, examines the bodies of Australian and Ottoman soldiers killed in the fighting.

Ottoman prisoners being interrogated by British soldiers.

British soldiers who suffered frostbite recover, lying on hay in a shelter made from biscuit boxes in Suvla Bay, Gallipoli, in November 1915.

This image was taken shortly before the evacuation of Anzac. Here, Australian troops attack a Turkish trench during the Dardanelles Campaign. However, they found the position empty, as the Turks had abandoned it.

W Beach (Lancashire Landing) at Cape Helles, Gallipoli, 7 January 1916, shortly before the final evacuation of British forces during the Battle of Gallipoli. In the background, on the left, it is possible to see the explosion of a Turkish bomb into the water, fired from the Asian coast of the Dardanelles.

A French 75mm gun in action near Sedd el Bahr during the third battle of Krithia, fought on 4 June 1915 as part of the Gallipoli Campaign.

Greek children next to the bones of soldiers killed in 1915 during the Gallipoli Campaign. The photo was taken in 1919 by Lieutenant Ernest Brooks.

GORLICE-TARNÓW OFFENSIVE | MAY 1 – SEPTEMBER 18 |

Initially, this offensive was considered a German action to ease Russia's pressure on the Austro-Hungarians on the Eastern Front, but it ended up resulting in the total ruin of the Russian lines. The continuous series of actions began in May and only came to an end in September, due to bad weather.

Russian prisoners of war after the battle.

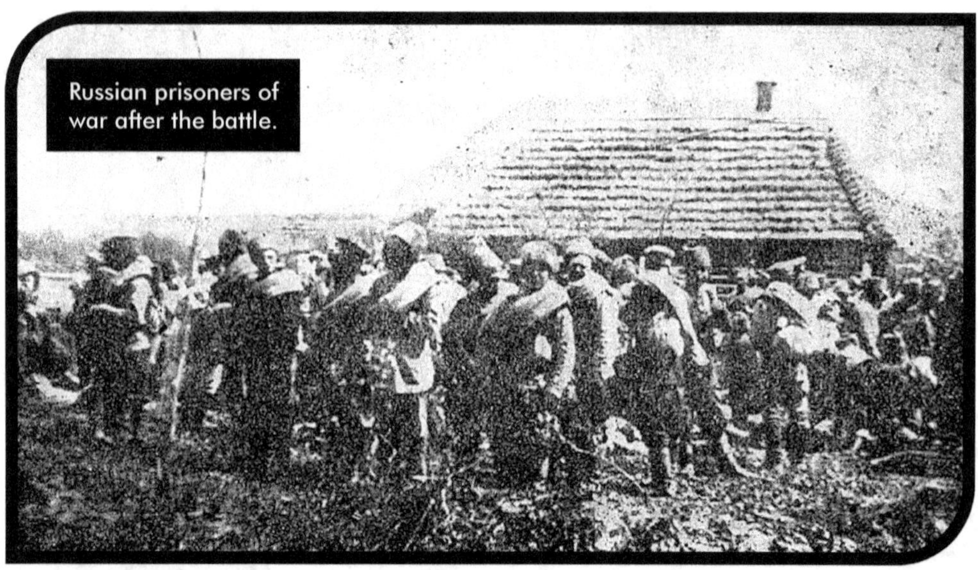

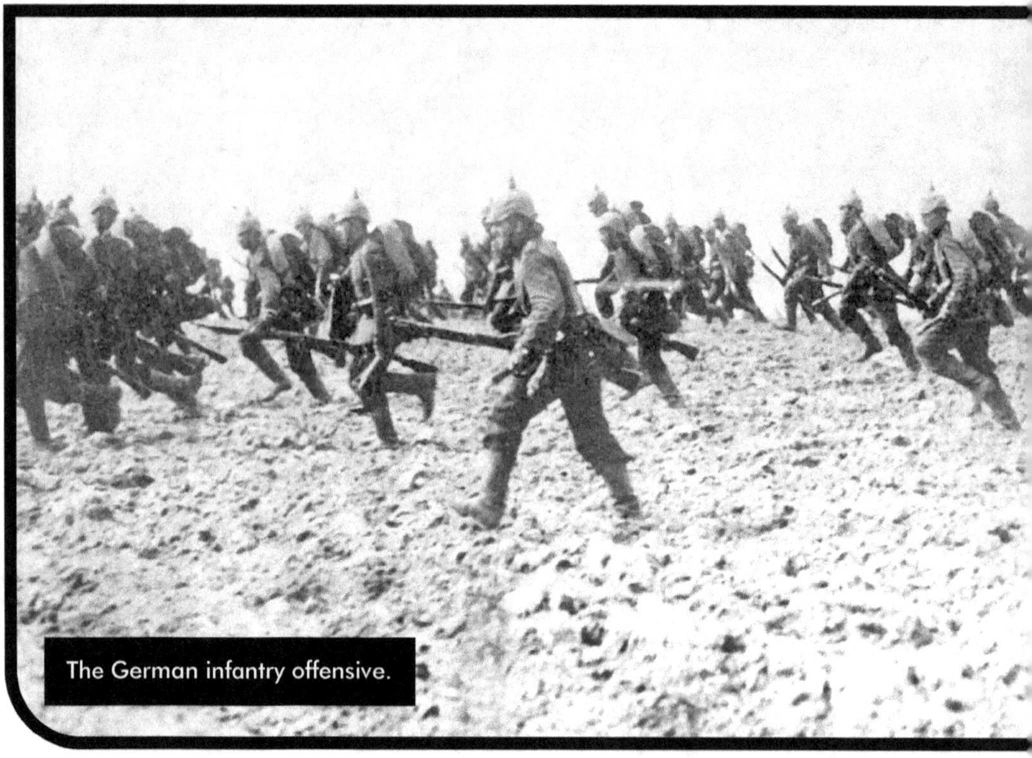

The German infantry offensive.

Wounded Russians going to the rear: ambulances were rare in Russia and the wounded often had to travel for two or three days in peasant carts to field hospitals.

Radko Dimitriev, commander of the Russian 3rd Army.

In the Second Battle of Artois, the Allies aimed to recapture a defensive position established in 1914 by the Germans between Rheims and Amiens, which threatened communications between Paris and northern France. A French advance into Artois could cut the railway lines supplying the German armies between Arras and Rheims.

The battle was fought during the German offensive of the Second Battle of Ypres. The initial French attack broke through and captured Mount Vimy, but reserve units were unable to reinforce the troops on the ridge, and German counterattacks forced them to withdraw.

British attacks on Festubert forced the Germans to retreat two miles, at the cost of many casualties on both sides. On June 18, the main offensive was stopped. The French offensive advanced about 1,8 miles, having fired 2,155,862 warheads, and lost 102,500 soldiers. In turn, the German 6th Army lost 73 thousand men.

The fierce fight between the Germans and the French to take the high ground at Loretto-Höhe.

On March 11, Major Hermann von der Lieth-Thomsen was appointed Chief of the German Air Forces, forming five new air units in Germany to provide replacements and accelerate the introduction of the new Fokker EI aircraft.

The taking of Carency village.

The once bucolic Carency.

The ruins of Carency.

FIRST BATTLE OF ISONZO | JUNE 23 – JULY 7 |

This clash involved Italy and Austria-Hungary in the Italian Campaign of World War I. The Italian forces intended to repel the Austrians away from their defensive positions at Soca (Isonzo). Although the Italians had a numerical superiority of 2 soldiers to 1, their offensive failed, since the Austrians had the advantage of fighting in high positions, blocked with barbed wire, which were able to easily resist enemy attacks.

In the following years, there were 11 more battles between the Austro-Hungarian and Italian armies in the region, where the territory of present-day Slovenia is and along the Isonzo River in the eastern sector of the Italian Front between June 1915 and November 1917.

The Isonzo River in Gorizia with the destroyed railway bridge.

Austro-Hungarian trenches in Soca (Isonzo).

BATTLE OF WARSAW | AUGUST 17 – SEPTEMBER 14 |

Also known as the Great Russian Retreat, it began when the forces of the Russian Empire withdrew from Galicia and Poland. On July 13, the entire Russian army managed to withdraw, leaving only a small contingent in Warsaw and the Ivangorod fortress, which was also captured by the German army.

The German cavalry enters Warsaw, on August 5, 1915.

A Russian rearguard trench during withdrawal.

BATTLE OF LOOS

The Battle of Loos was one of the major British offensives on the Western Front in 1915. It was the first time the British used poison gas during the war.

British infantry advances through mustard gas at Loos, 25 September 1915.

SECOND BATTLE OF CHAMPAGNE

The result of this battle was disastrous for the French who, after some offensives and counter-offensives by the Germans, lost all the positions they had conquered, in addition to having suffered 145 thousand casualties, half the number of enemy deaths.

Distribution of bread to German prisoners, September 26.

French Army leader Joseph Joffre (left) in conversation with Fernand de Langle de Cary (center) and Adolphe Guillaumat.

Frontline trenches in Champagne (1915).

Logistics is an essential element to guarantee victory in major battles. This picture shows the French refueling station at Sainte-Menehould, during the Battle of Champagne.

Artillery preparation, 220mm mortars, during the combat on September 26.

War Aviation

The first aerial battle of the war – and also the first in history – was fought during the Battle of Monte Cer still in 1914. The engagement took place when a Serbian aviator, Miodrag Tomić, was carrying out aerial reconnaissance over enemy positions. Tomić crossed paths with an Austro-Hungarian plane. The pilot waved and Tomić returned the salute. But, although the initial gesture was courteous, the Austro-Hungarian pilot took out his revolver and began shooting at the Serb. Tomić managed to escape. The episode, however, led to an innovation: within a few weeks, all planes, both from the Allies and the Central Powers, were equipped with machine guns, initially above the wings.

One of the first attempts to mount a machine gun on the bow of a French Morane-Saulnier L.

This image shows the first armed plane of the Serbian Army, in 1915. The plane is Bleriot XI-2, the pilot is Tomić and the observer is Mihajlović. The Cyrillic characters, in Latin letters OLUJ, mean "storm." The Serbs were among the first to arm their planes for aerial combat.

Bulgarian soldiers in position to fire at an approaching plane on the Southern Front.

Autochrome of a
Nieuport fighter in
Aisne, France (c. 1916).

Fokker M.5K/MG military
serial number "E.5/15"
of the German forces.

The slow-moving B.E.2c continued
in service until 1916; although it
was stable, it was considered a
"flying target" for German pilots.

WOMEN IN THE WAR

The Girl Behind the Gun

The War Budget,
December 30th, 1915.

This page from the December 30, 1915, issue of English War magazine shows British women working in munitions factories. The above picture shows an installation of covers on the pumps. Below is final inspection of the warheads.

The Girl Tommy Atkins left behind him has enlisted in the great Munition Corps with "barracks" all over the country. There are now few processes in shell and cartridge manufacture with which women cannot be trusted. Above, percussion caps are being fitted, and below is a section of the testing room, where girls are gauging the shell cases as they pass along on a travelling belt.

"

"Women are working day and night to win the war" (Witherby & Co. London. 1915): a poster urging women to participate in the British war effort, published in the *Young Women's Christian Association* magazine.

German women working in the war effort (c. 1917): Western Front communications assistants on their way to work.

BATTLE OF VERDUN

One of the main clashes of the First World War on the Western Front brought the German army and French troops face to face on steep terrain north of the city of Verdun-sur-Meuse, northeast of France. It was the longest battle of the First World War and military history, and one of the most devastating in terms of casualties. Although exact numbers are not available, it is estimated that 714,321 men lost their lives in the battle – 377,231 on the French side and 337,000 on the German side.

French troops attack
under artillery fire,
in the Fleury ravine.

French battery fires on
German forces in Verdun.

Execution of a French deserter in Verdun.

The battlefield in Verdun, seen from the Fort de la Chaume.

Verdun, as imagined by
Félix Vallotton (1865-1925).

Reserves crossing a river
on the way to Verdun.
"They will not pass" is a
phrase that will always be
associated with the heroic
defense of Verdun.

BATTLE OF BITLIS

The Battle of Bitlis was, in fact, a series of clashes that took place during the summer of 1916, in the city of Bitlis, in present-day Turkey, between Russian and Ottoman forces. Bitlis was conquered by the Russians on March 2, 1916, with the support of Armenian volunteers. Immediately, the Ottomans, under the command of Kemal Atatürk, began a reaction and retook Bitlis on August 15, after expelling Nikolai Yudenitch's army. The Turkish counterattack was only stopped at Gevash on August 24. Bitlis was the first battle in which the Ottoman Army was successful against the Russians.

Ottoman forces commanded by Kemal Atatürk in Bitlis.

Mustafa Kemal Atatürk (1881 - 1938), a soldier and revolutionary who demonstrated his talents in the First World War, was the founder of the Republic of Turkey. As Turkey's first president, Atatürk launched a program of political, economic, and cultural reforms, seeking to transform the ruins of the Ottoman Empire into a democratic and secular nation. The principles of Atatürk's reforms, called "Kemalism," remain the political foundation of the modern Turkish state.

Mustafa Kemal Atatürk as the Army Commander.

Russian troops and Armenian volunteers under the command of Colonel Antranik, Armenian national hero, marching into Bitlis. Antranik was decorated by the Russian government for his part in the capture of Bitlis.

BATTLE OF JUTLAND | MAY 31 – JUNE 1 |

It was the largest naval battle of the Great War, as well as the only – therefore, last – large-scale battle among battleships in the conflict. Some historians believe that the battle between British and German fleets off the coast of the Jutland peninsula in Denmark was the largest naval battle ever seen. It cannot be said that there was a winner, as both sides suffered serious losses. However, with the damage to the German fleet, the British continued to control the sea.

The 2nd Division of the Grand Fleet Squadron: King George V followed by Thunderer, Monarch, and Conqueror.

The explosion of the HMS Queen Mary ship in the Battle of Jutland.

The firing of a German torpedo.

Reinhard Scheer, commander of the German fleet.

Franz Hipper, commander of the German cruiser squadron.

John Jellicoe, commander of the British fleet.

David Beatty, commander
of the British cruiser fleet.

HMS Warspite and
Malaysia, seen from HMS
Valiant at around 2 p.m.

The third turret of the cruiser Lion was hit by a 12-inch shell, which pierced the turret at the junction of the armor plate and detonated above the gun barrel.

Beatty's flagship Lion catches fire after being hit by a salvo from the Lützow.

The HMS Indefatigable sinks after being hit by gunfire from the German cruiser Von der Tann.

The explosion of HMS Queen Mary.

The Invincible explodes after being hit by the Lützow and Derfflinger's cannons.

The HMS Birmingham in flames.

The SMS Seydlitz was heavily damaged in the battle, hit by 21 rounds from the main guns, several of the secondary caliber guns, and by one torpedo. 98 men were killed and 55 were wounded.

A crew member of the SMS Westfalen.

BATTLE OF DOBERDÒ | AUGUST 6 |

One of the bloodiest battlefields of the Great War was also the sixth of the 12 battles of the Isonzo. The confrontation involved the Italian and Austro-Hungarian armies. The Italians attempted to advance on the Carso Plateau, seeking to gain control over the main road linking the port of Trieste to the city of Gorizia. After fierce fighting and enormous casualties, they were successful in their attempts. The Austro-Hungarian forces retreated and Gorizia fell to the Italians. They, however, were unable to continue the advance to Trieste, being stopped near Duino.

A Batalha de Doberdó, entre o exército italiano e austro-húngaro, por R.A. Höger (1873-1930).

BRUSILOV OFFENSIVE | JUNE 4 – SEPTEMBER 20 |

It was the greatest achievement of the Russian Empire during the First World War and one of the cruelest battles in history, considered by some scholars as the greatest victory of the Triple Entente. The great assault against the armies of the Central Empires on the Eastern Front promoted by the Russians took place in what is now Ukrainian territory. It received its name from a southwestern front commander, Aleksei Brusilov (1853 - 1926), who developed the strategies that guaranteed Russian victory.

Austro-Hungarian soldiers handing over Russian troops on the Romanian border.

The Russian Military Council on April 1, 1916: generals Ivanov (in the right corner with a beard), Klimovsky, Brusilov (with a white mustache), Tsar Nicholas II (in the center), generals Kuropatkin, Sievers and Pustovoitenko, the Minister of War Shuvayev, and generals Alekseyev and Evert.

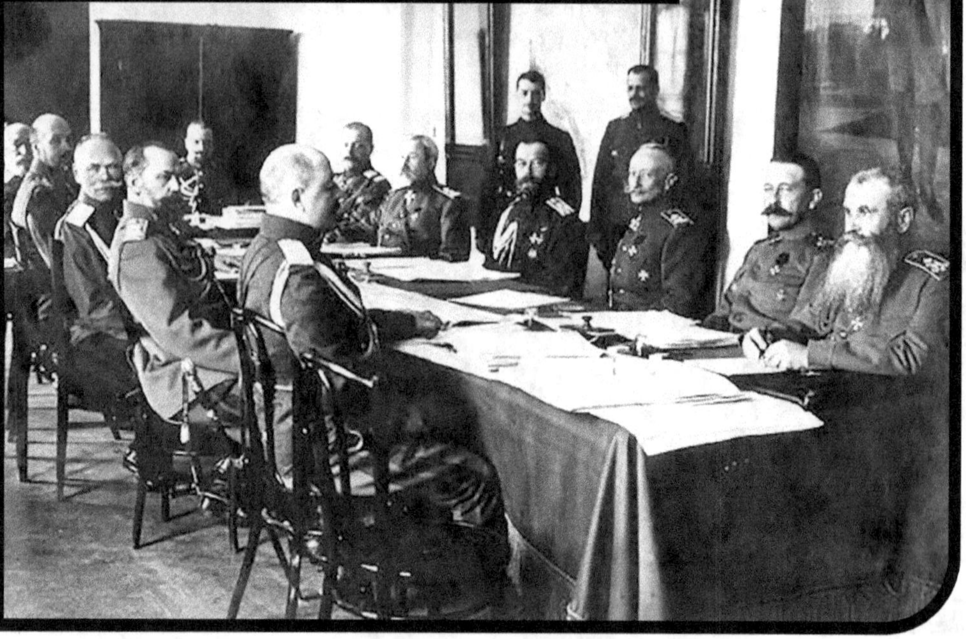

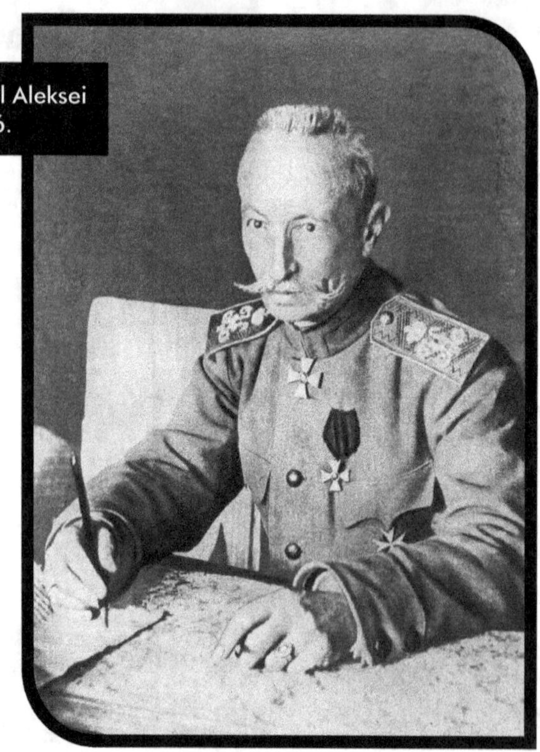

Russian General Aleksei Brusilov in 1916.

BATTLE OF THE SOMME

The Anglo-French offensive aimed to break through the German defense lines stationed in the Somme River region, in France. The casualties were significant for both sides, especially for Great Britain. On the first day alone, the British suffered 57,470 casualties (19,240 dead) – the bloodiest combat in the history of the British army. In total, the battle resulted in more than 1.2 million victims, including dead and wounded, in five months of combat, in one of the most violent military operations in the history of humanity.

Members of the 1st Battalion of the Royal Irish Rifles in a communications trench, on the first day of operations on the Somme, 1916.

French President Raymond Poincaré and Marshal Joseph Joffre visit the front during the Battle of the Somme in 1916.

British wounded near Bernafay Wood (July 1916), during the Battle of the Somme. A German prisoner helps an enemy soldier on his way to a medical station in the Bernafay Forest.

British infantry from the Wiltshire Regiment attacking near Thiepval, on 7 August 1916, during the Battle of the Somme.

A German trench occupied by men of the 11th Battalion of the Cheshire Regiment near the Albert-Bapaume Road at Ovillers-la-Boisselle, July 1916, during the Battle of the Somme.

Public Schools Battalion (16th Battalion, the Middlesex Regiment) made up of volunteer teachers and staff.

Vickers machine gun crew wearing gas masks near Ovillers, in July 1916.

Men of the Royal Warwickshire Regiment rest exhausted at the rear of the action.

Royal Garrison Artillery eight-inch howitzers, in action in the Fricourt-Mametz Valley, August 1916, during the Battle of the Somme. A howitzer is a type of cannon with a relatively short tube that fires explosive projectiles in curved trajectories.

BATTLE OF FROMELLES

This British military operation on the Western Front was also known as part of the Battle of the Somme. Preparations for the clash were made hastily, the troops involved were inexperienced in trench warfare and the strength of the German defense was greatly underestimated – one British soldier for two Germans. As a result, the German counterattack forced the withdrawal of Australian troops to the original front line.

British soldiers killed in a German toxic gas attack on June 19 during the Battle of Fromelles.

The Fokker E.III Eindecker used in battle.

Members of the 53rd Australian Battalion. Only three men from this battalion survived the battle; even so, they were wounded.

A German bunker at Fromelles.

BATTLE OF POZIÈRES | JULY 23 – AUGUST 7 |

The two-week fight for the French village of Pozières marked the middle stages of the Battle of the Somme. Although British divisions were involved in most phases of the battle, Pozières is mainly remembered as a fight fought by the Australians who, at a huge cost in terms of lives, achieved their objective.

The view across the Pozières plateau during the battle.

The "Gibraltar" bunker, Pozières, at the end of August. A tired group loaded with sandbags marches to the fight at Mouquet Farm.

The road to Pozières: in the background, the village of Contalmaison is under fire from German artillery.

The view across the battlefield towards Mouquet Farm from a British trench.

Postcard with Australian soldiers carrying a 9.45mm cannon on the Pozières plateau. The gunners were identified, from left to right, as: Sergeant Daley; Albert Roy Kyle; Clift, gunner Lear, and gunner Clive Talbot.

BATTLE OF GUILLEMONT | SEPTEMBER 3 – 6 |

It was a British assault on the village of the same name, controlled by the Germans during the Battle of the Somme. On September 3, the British captured Guillemont and, two days later, Falfemont Farm. The German units involved fought to the death in the trenches. The capture of Guillemont weakened German control over this sector, allowing the British to launch their next major offensive on a broad front.

A German bunker with bed: the British were impressed by the comfort available to enemy soldiers.

The main street
of Guillemont
after the battle.

A 9.2-inch howitzer in Carnoy
Valley, during the battle.

German artillery returning fire.

The Albatros C.III observation plane used at Guillemont.

A S.S. class airship.

BATTLE OF GINCHY

The conquest of the village of Ginchy by the United Kingdom's 16th Irish Division took a heavy toll on the Allies. The Irish suffered heavy casualties during the fighting: the seven Irish battalions involved in the battle lost eight officers and 220 men, of which six officers and 61 men belonged to the 9th Battalion of the Royal Dublin Fusiliers, which lost the largest number of combatants. The sacrifice guaranteed an advantage for the Allies. The successful attack, which captured the village on the first attempt, deprived the Germans of their strategic observation posts.

British battery in Contalmaison.

German 6-inch howitzers.

Troops advance in the Battle of Ginchy.

Aerial reconnaissance camera, operated by the pilot of a B.E.2c.

A German soldier during the operations in Ginchy.

MONASTIR OFFENSIVE | SEPTEMBER 12 – DECEMBER 11 |

The Allied assault was intended to once and for all defeat the forces of the Central Powers on the Macedonian Front, forcing Bulgaria's capitulation and relieving pressure on Romania. The offensive lasted three months, and after the capture of the city of Monastir, it came to an end.

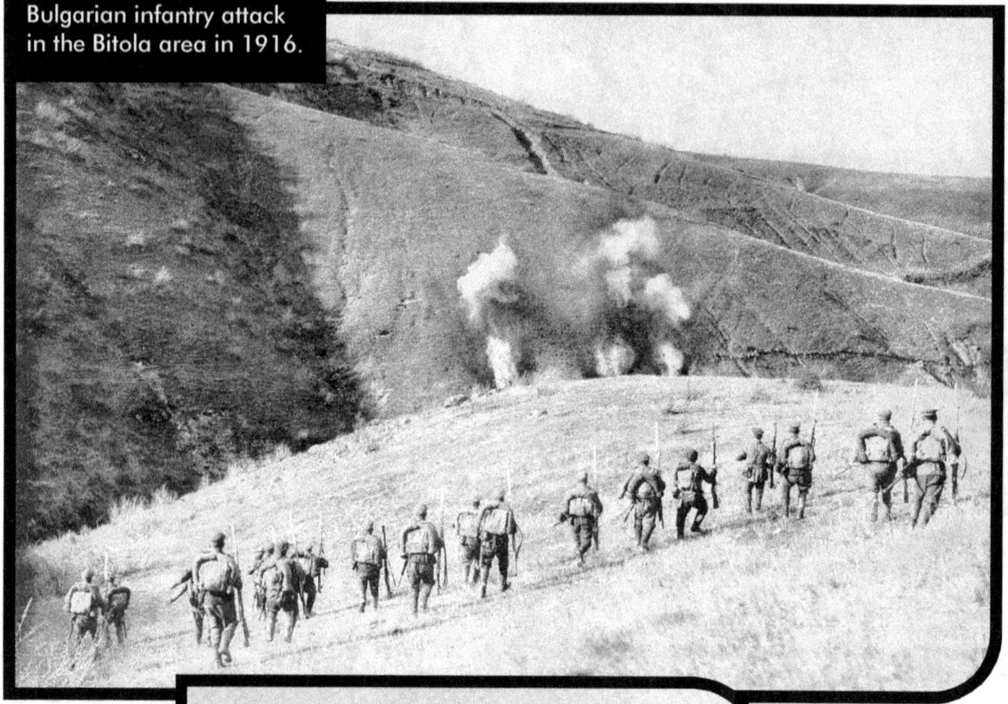

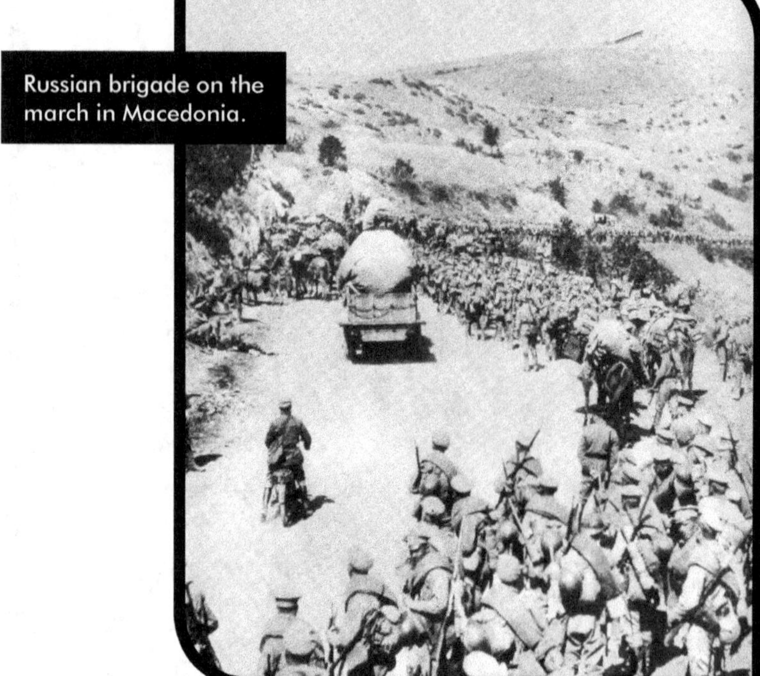

Bulgarian infantry attack in the Bitola area in 1916.

Russian brigade on the march in Macedonia.

Withdrawal of the Serbian army towards Albania.

Serbian troops in retreat in the winter of 1915/16.

Exhausted Serbian soldiers wait for allied ships to rescue them in February 1916.

French gunners with a 75mm anti-aircraft gun in Thessaloniki.

1917

THE US ENTRY INTO THE WAR

The Allies received decisive reinforcement with the entry of the United States into the war in April 1917. The country sent 2.1 million soldiers, which allowed new offensives: the Second Battle of the Marne and the Hundred Days Offensive. The action included six hundred war tanks and the support of eight hundred planes. The offensives resulted in the collapse of German forces, already exhausted after four years of fighting.

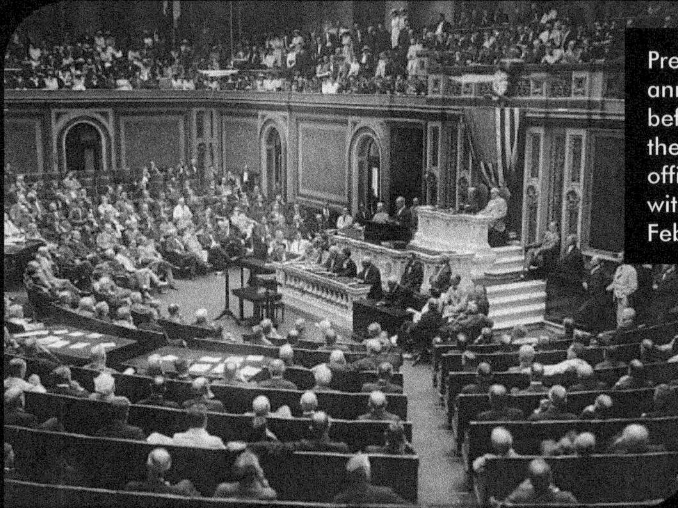

President Wilson announces, before Congress, the severing of official relations with Germany, on February 3, 1917.

Volunteers register by responding to the draft in New York, in June 1917.

The famous American propaganda poster for recruitment: "Uncle Sam Needs You," by James Montgomery Flagg.

American troops advance uphill on the Western Front.

Americans on the battlefield during World War I.

US soldiers wearing gas masks.

MIDDLE EASTERN THEATER

The theater in which the Ottoman Empire became involved was the Middle Eastern one, where it mainly faced the Russians and the British. The French and British moved the Gallipoli campaign in 1915 and the Mesopotamia campaign the following year. However, after being defeated at the Siege of Kut, the British reorganized and managed to reconquer Baghdad in March 1917. After victory in the Romani Battle in August 1916, the British Empire's Egyptian Expeditionary Force advanced through the Sinai Peninsula, defeating the Ottoman army in the Battles of Magdhaba and Rafah, in Egyptian Sinai and Ottoman Palestine. The Arab Revolt, started in 1916 and supported by the British, freed the Arabian Peninsula from Ottoman rule. Several nomadic tribes led by Hussein bin Ali and supported by the British ended up taking Mecca.

British troops enter Baghdad (March 1917), with Sir Frederick Stanley Maude leading the Indian army.

British forces on the march in Mesopotamia.

British artillery battery during the Battle of Jerusalem in 1917.

The Turkish trenches on the shores of the Dead Sea.

Kurdish cavalry troops.

THE TURKISH MASSACRE AGAINST THE ARMENIANS

The genocide of Armenians by the Ottoman Empire was the first modern genocide. Right at the beginning of the War, officers of the Armed Forces called "Young Turks" took over the administration of the Ottoman government in 1908, and began to consider the Armenian population as enemies, since these people supported Russia (the greatest enemy of Turks) at the beginning of the war, even fighting alongside the Russians. The government saw this fact as a pretext to grant a Deportation Law, authorizing the removal of the entire Armenian population from the eastern provinces of the empire to Syria, between 1915 and 1917. The deportations were, in fact, a pretext for cruel mass executions. Although the exact number of victims is unknown, it is estimated that between 250,000 and 1.5 million Armenian men, women, and children were executed.

An Armenian mother beside the bodies of her five children.

The corpses of Muslims who were arrested in the Armenian neighborhood of Erzincan and burned alive on February 12, 1918, are transported to a cemetery during the Caucasus Campaign.

Victims of the Armenian genocide.

BATTLE OF ARRAS | APRIL 9 – MAY 16 |

It was a British offensive that included British, Canadian, New Zealand, Newfoundland, and Australian troops. The Allies attacked German defenses near the French city of Arras, on the Western Front. When the battle officially ended on May 16, the troops of the British Empire had advanced significantly on the ground, but had not been able to penetrate the German defenses – the main purpose of the attack.

German troops with a captured British tank on April 11, near Bullecourt.

BATTLE OF VIMY RIDGE | APRIL 9 – 12 |

This combat was part of the opening phase of the British-led Battle of Arras, an attack carried out to support the Nivelle Offensive. The Canadian Corps' objective was the capture and control of the high ground. The Canadians captured most of the hill during the first day of the attack. The city of Thélus was taken during the second day of the attack. The last objective, a small position outside the town of Givenchy-en-Gohelle, was captured on 12 April. German forces withdrew from the Oppy–Méricourt line, opening space for the Allied advance.

A Batalha de Vimy, pintura de Richard Jack.

BATTLE OF MESSINES | JUNE 7 – 14 |

A prelude to the Third Battle of Ypres, this offensive was commanded by the British Second Army. The action forced the German army to mobilize its reserves from the Arras and Aisne fronts to Flanders, which took some pressure off the French Army.

An Australian truck during a bombing in Messines.

BATTLE OF PASSCHENDAELE OR THIRD BATTLE OF YPRES
| JULY 31 – NOVEMBER 6 |

The Third Battle of Ypres, also called the Battle of Passchendaele, pitted the British, as well as their Canadian, South African allies, and units of the Australian and New Zealand Armed Forces (ANZAC), against forces of the German Empire, in a dispute for the region surrounding the Belgian city of Ypres. Passchendaele is situated on the last hill east of Ypres, close to a railway junction at Roulers, a vital part of the German 4th Army's supply system, which the British and their allies were expected to take. The campaign ended in November when the Canadian Corps finally captured Passchendaele.

A French observation post.

German prisoners.

Smoke screen.

Canadian soldiers carry a howitzer.

Members of the Royal Marine Artillery load a 15-inch howitzer near the Menin road during the Third Battle of Ypres.

An underground shelter near Hooge Crater during the third battle of Ypres.

"Bringing Up the Guns," oil on canvas by Harold Power (1917), depicts soldiers from the 101st Australian Battery carrying cannons during the Battle of Passchendaele. The image conveys the difficulties that the British and Australian artillerymen faced in a terrain so disturbed by incessant bombing that transporting weapons after each advance ended up becoming a superhuman effort.

This composite photograph, a postcard from the "Our Boys at the Front" series, shows a bayonet charge by Australian troops and biplanes at Passchendaele.

The Private John "Barney" Hines of the Australian 45th Battalion, surrounded by looted German equipment during the battle of Polygon Wood, part of the Passchendaele campaign, in September 1917. He is counting the money stolen from German prisoners of war, among the enemy's weapons and personal equipment.

British soldiers carry a cannon through the mud near Zillebeke, 9 August 1917.

Ypres Campaign, Battle of Poelcappelle: men handling 18-pounder through mud near Langemarck, 16 October 1917.

Australian troops amid the devastation of war, in Ypres.

A mule train gets stuck in the mud near Potijze Farm, Ypres: mud was a major problem faced by soldiers fighting in the Third Battle of Ypres.

Soldiers of the 4th Division Artillery passing through Chateau Wood, near Hooge in the Ypres salient, on 29 October 1917. The castle was bombed on 31 October 1914, when all members of the three British divisions using it as barracks were killed. The ruins were reconquered several times by both the Germans and the Allies. Hooge is currently a memorial.

BATTLE OF MĂRĂȘEȘTI | AUGUST 6 – SEPTEMBER 8 |

The Battle of Mărăşeşti was the last major battle between the German Empire and the Kingdom of Romania on the Romanian front. Romania was occupied by the Central Powers, but the battle of Mărăşeşti ensured that the northeastern region of the country remained free from occupation.

Romanian troops during the battle of Mărăşeşti.

Marshal Joseph Joffre, commander of the French army in World War I, during the years 1914 to 1916, inspecting Romanian troops.

RUSSIA'S EXIT FROM THE WAR

After the October Revolution of 1917, when the Bolsheviks took power, Russia was weakened by internal crises and by its participation in the international conflict raging in Europe. To carry out social-economic recovery and development plans, which included a free healthcare system for the entire population, the guarantee of women's rights, and the end of illiteracy, the new Bolshevik government had to first take Russia out of the First World War. To this end, the Russian authorities signed the disadvantageous Treaty of Brest-Litovsk, under which Russia lost important territories to Germany, such as Estonia, Lithuania, Ukraine, and Finland.

A caricature of Mikhail Romanov, brother of Tsar Nicholas II and commander of the Wild Division, a corps of volunteers, at the beginning of 1917, reproduced in the Russian press after the February Revolution, plays with the demotivation of the empire's soldiers. The Adjutant General, the Grand Duke, asks the commander: "Are you sure, Mikhail? The Army is on strike today!"

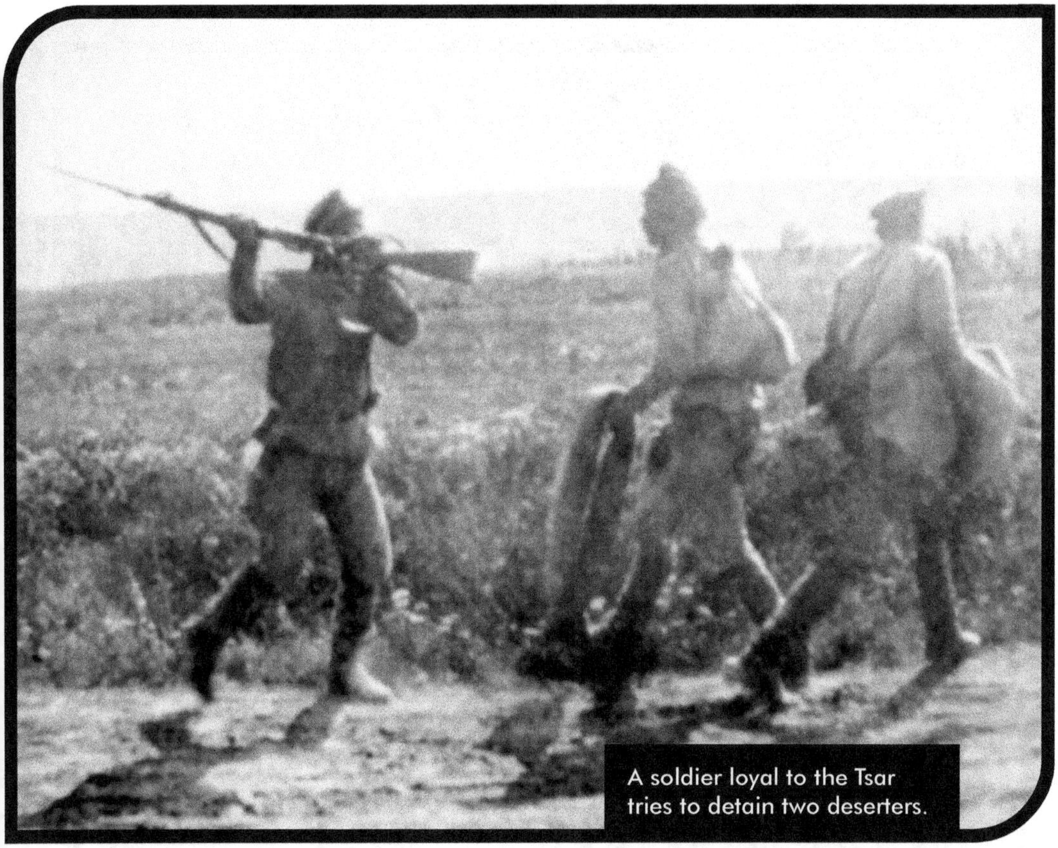

A soldier loyal to the Tsar tries to detain two deserters.

Battle of Galicia Lubok.

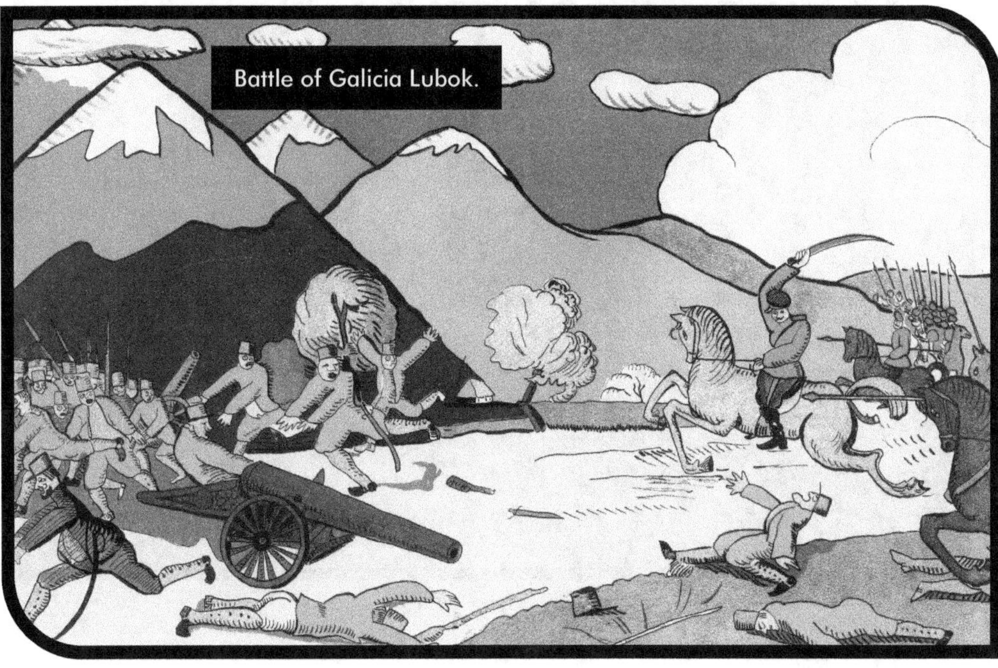

A Russian armored vehicle (c. 1917).

The signing of the Treaty of Brest-Litovski on February 9, 1918.

1918

THE VARDAR OFFENSIVE

The offensive was carried out during the final phase of the Balkan Campaign, when on September 15, a combined force of Serbian, French, and Greek troops attacked Bulgarian trenches at Dobro Pole, in today's Republic of Macedonia. The artillery fire before the attack had devastating effects on the morale of the Bulgarians and eventually led to mass desertions. Although the Bulgarians then managed to halt the Allied advance in the Doiran sector, the collapse of the Dobro Pole front forced the defenders to withdraw from Doiran. The offensive led Bulgaria to sign the Armistice of Salonica and withdraw from the war. The fall of Bulgaria turned the strategic and operational balance of the war against the Central Powers.

German soldiers on the Crna River in Macedonia in 1918.

A Bulgarian telephone station with trench periscope observing the enemy's position on the Doiran front.

British forces in the Thessalonica Campaign fire a 18-pounder from a camouflaged position on the Doiran Front.

SPRING OFFENSIVE | MARCH 21 – JULY 18 |

In 1918, with Russia's withdrawal from the conflict, marking the end of the war in the east, the Germans were able to employ the forces released on the eastern front on the western front. Because of this, they launched the Spring Offensive. Using new infiltration tactics, the Germans advanced about 100 km west – the largest advance made by any army on the Western Front. The Spring Offensive was nearly successful in breaking through the Allied lines. These, however, managed to resist.

Soldiers from the British 55th (West Lancashire) Division injured by tear gas await treatment at a medical outpost near Bethune during the battle of Estaires on 10 April 1918, part of the German offensive in Flanders.

A German A7V tank at Roye, on March 21, 1918, the first day of the Spring Offensive.

Portuguese prisoners of war.

German prisoners in the custody of Australian troops, April 23, 1918.

Germans passing through a trench captured by the British.

BATTLE OF THE LYS | APRIL 9 – 29 |

Fought during the Spring Offensive, this confrontation negatively marked Portugal's participation in the First World War. The defeat that the German armies inflicted on the Portuguese troops was the country's greatest military disaster after the Battle of Alcácer-Quibir, in 1578.

Trenches in the Lys.

SECOND BATTLE OF THE MARNE |MAY 27 – AUGUST 6|

Also called the Battle of Reims, it was the last significant German thrust on the Western Front. However, the Allied counterattack, under the command of French forces and counting hundreds of tanks, neutralized the German action, inflicting heavy casualties. The defeat of the German soldiers began the relentless advance of the Allies in the so-called Hundred Days Offensive, which ended in the armistice.

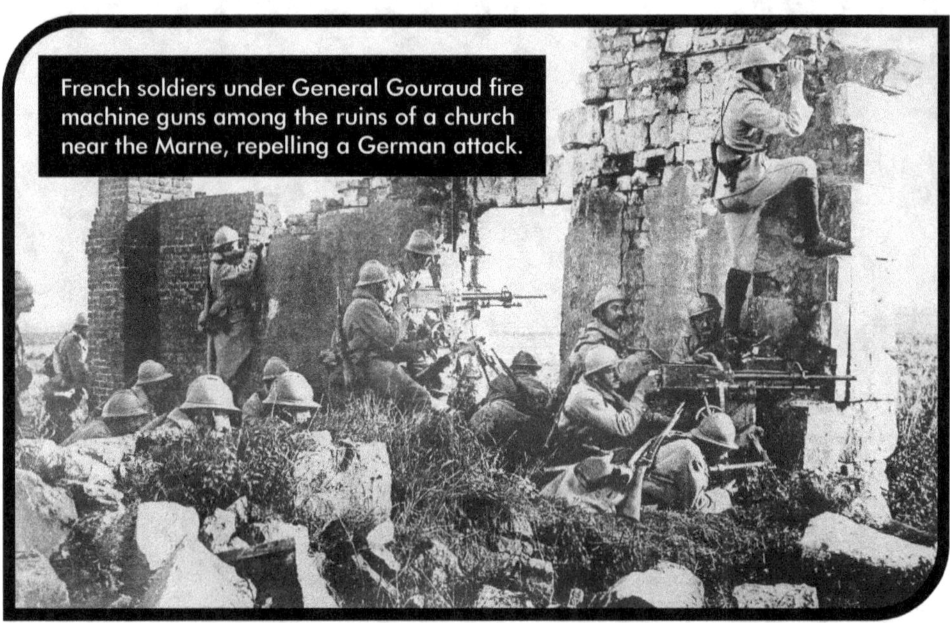

French soldiers under General Gouraud fire machine guns among the ruins of a church near the Marne, repelling a German attack.

The aerial view of ruins at Vaux-devant-Damloup, France, in 1918.

An American major piloting an observation balloon near the front: the US participation in the war, providing material resources and large numbers of men, allowed the Allies to launch new and decisive offensives against the Germans.

French soldiers launch a toxic gas attack on German trenches in Flanders, Belgium.

Germans killed in the La Basse area.

BATTLE OF AMIENS | AUGUST 8 – 11 |

Also called the Third Battle of Picardy, the action marked the beginning of the Hundred Days Offensive, which would bring about the end of the First World War. Allied forces advanced about 7 miles on the first day, one of the greatest advances of the war, under the command of English general Baron Henry Rawlinson. Amiens was one of the first major battles involving armored vehicles and brought an end to trench warfare on the Western Front. A significant number of Germans surrendered, indicating the shaken spirits of the Kaiser's soldiers.

"Amiens, the key of the west" by Arthur Streeton, 1918.

HUNDRED DAYS OFFENSIVE | AGUST 8 – NOVEMBER 11 |

The United States' entry into the war provided the allies with the reinforcement they needed. The country sent 2.1 million soldiers, which allowed a new and major action that put an end to the war: the Hundred Days Offensive. The operation included 600 tanks, in addition to the support of 800 planes. The German soldiers, overcome by exhaustion after four years of fighting, were defeated. Faced with the relentless advance of the Allies in 1918, German military leaders were certain that defeat was inevitable and sought an armistice.

A machine gun post established by the Australian 54th Battalion during the attack on German forces in the town of Somme.

The introduction of thousands of tanks along the front was an innovation developed by the Allies as a strategy to overcome the stalemate of trench warfare on the Western Front. In the image, a French Renault FT tank passes a trench.

Canadian troops sheltering in a ditch along the Arras-Cambrai Road: horses alongside tanks testify to a world in transition.

BATTLE OF MEGIDO | SEPTEMBER 19 – 21 |

This battle made possible the conquest of Palestine by the British, under the command of Edmund Allenby. The Ottomans were surrounded by British Empire forces in the Jezreel Valley, near the Jordan River, achieving victory with very few casualties.

A group of German prisoners captured during fighting at Semakh on the Sea of Galilee.

MEUSE–ARGONNE OFFENSIVE | SEPTEMBER 26 – NOVEMBER 11 |

Part of the Hundred Days Offensive, this operation was the largest and most significant of the American Expeditionary Force (AEF) in World War I. The planning was carried out by French commander Ferdinand Foch and involved forces from the USA, France, the United Kingdom, Commonwealth countries, and Belgium. The objective was to break the Hindenburg Line, the great defense system built by the Germans during the winter of 1916-1917 in northeastern France, forcing the Germans to capitulate, an aim that was successfully accomplished.

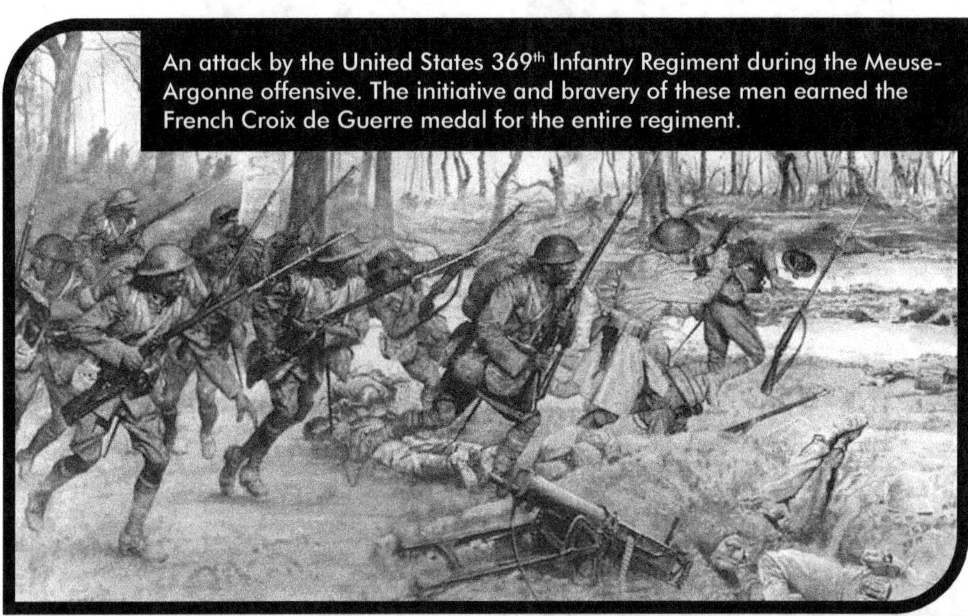

An attack by the United States 369th Infantry Regiment during the Meuse-Argonne offensive. The initiative and bravery of these men earned the French Croix de Guerre medal for the entire regiment.

A German Hannover CL III plane shot down between Montfaucon and Cierges on October 4, 1918.

Ruins after the Battle of Montfaucon.

Men of the 16th Canadian Infantry Battalion during the Battle of the Canal du Nord, part of the Hundred Days Offensive.

BATTLE OF CAMBRAI | OCTOBER 8 – 10 |

The French city gave its name to the battle that resulted in British and German troops clashing. The battle was notable for the inauguration of several innovative tactics and weapons, especially the use of tanks, which resulted in a crushing victory for the Allies with few casualties.

British soldiers with a tank in the background: the use of this new weapon was decisive in the Battle of Cambrai.

The "no man's land," the free stretch between the trenches near Lens, France.

BATTLE OF VITTORIO VENETO | OCTOBER 24 – NOVEMBER 4 |

The last Italian campaign of the Great War led Italy to victory and the Austro-Hungarian army to collapse.

Italian and British troops pass artillery pieces abandoned by the Austro-Hungarians on the Val d'Assa mountain road, November 2, 1918.

BATTLE OF SHARQAT | OCTOBER 23 – 30 |

The confrontation between British forces and the Ottoman Empire as part of the Mesopotamian Campaign was the final engagement of the Turks, who agreed to an armistice upon being defeated.

Trenches during the Siege of Kut, in the Mesopotamian Campaign.

THE END OF THE WAR

The Treaty of Versailles was not a peace agreement, as the document's harsh conditions imposed on the newly proclaimed Weimar Republic hurt German pride. When presenting the treaty, the Allies reported that if the German government did not accept it, the war would resume. The head of the German government, Philipp Scheidemann, resigned, ceasing to sign the treaty. Gustav Bauer, leader of the coalition government that formed after Scheidemann's resignation, sent a telegram to Paris confirming his intention to sign the treaty if some articles were withdrawn. The allies' response came in an ultimatum: either Germany submitted to those conditions, or their armies would cross the Rhine within 24 hours and invade the country. Soon, the Germans were forced to accept a humiliation that would open the doors to Nazism and prepare the ground for the Second World War.

Men of the 7th Infantry Division of the 64th U.S. Regiment celebrated the news of the armistice on November 11, 1918.

Heads of State gathered for the signing of the treaty in the Hall of Mirrors, Versailles, June 28, 1919.

A German submarine (U-boat) U-155 displayed as a prize of war near the Tower Bridge, London, after the Armistice.